This is not the final v... an exceptionally use... without being simp... predictable. Useful w... without being prescriptive. Graham Beynon has done us all a huge favour in writing this, and I very much hope it helps provide an effective way into one of the most pressing and urgent needs of our day – the littering of our world with communities of light, a.k.a. churches!

Steve Timmis
Director of *Acts 29 Network* in Western Europe

This little book will introduce you to the many different ways that people go about planting churches. Given that the Church is God's chosen instrument to save the world, what could be more important than learning about how new churches can begin?

Adrian Warnock
blogger, adrianwarnock.com

Christians can easily ascribe to Graham Beynon's desire: 'to see God glorified by His gospel being spread and His church growing'. But we often do not see as He does – the consequence of such a desire: 'This will inevitably mean more churches and so church planting.' And even when we see that inevitability, we often do not see the complexities of the task. Graham has done a great service by teasing out some of the many issues involved in church planting. I warmly commend this book to all who would like to follow through on the inevitable outcome of their evangelistic desire.

Phillip Jensen
Dean of St Andrew's Cathedral, Sydney, Australia

An invaluable resource for laymen and professional clergy alike, Beynon's text is an essential guide for navi-gating the waters of church planting. Rife with resources essential to the development and cultivation of the church plant, Planting for the Gospel is a multi-faceted jewel that sparkles with ideas on church planting approaches, avenues, venues and systems.

J. Edward Norton
Minister of Evangelism and Global Church Planting,
Independent Presbyterian Church, Memphis, Tennessee

The goal of planting for the gospel is that Jesus would use us to build His church for His glory. Graham Beynon provides a series of preliminary ideas to encourage us to think of church planting as a fruitful means for making disciples and spreading the gospel. This resource is very helpful for mother churches to think strategically about planting a daughter church and also for young pastors to explore their calling in following the will of God as bearer of God's mission to people of all nations.

Scott Thomas
President, Acts 29 Network
Pastor of Global Church, Mars Hill Church, Seattle, Washington
Author and Creator of Gospel Coach

Planting for the Gospel

A hands-on guide to church planting

GRAHAM BEYNON

CHRISTIAN
FOCUS

Graham Beynon has experience of church planting having planted The Avenue Community Church in Leicester. He is currently studying for a PhD, acting as Course Director for 'Team' (Training for East Anglia Ministry) and involved in church ministry in Cambridge. He is married to Charis and they have three children.

Copyright © Graham Beynon

ISBN 978-1-84550-636-0

10 9 8 7 6 5 4 3 2 1

Published in 2011
by
Christian Focus Publications,
Geanies House, Fearn,
Ross-shire, IV20 1TW, Scotland
www.christianfocus.com

Cover design
by
Moose77.com

Printed by
Norhaven, Denmark

Contents

Section 1

Section 2

Dedication

This book is dedicated to Chris, Stu, Paul and
Pete: partners in plotting, planning and leading
a church plant. It's been one of my greatest
joys and privileges to work with you all.

SECTION 1

Introduction

One sunny April day, a group of people were standing nervously outside a school building. We were waiting for the caretaker to come and open up for us. He was late and I was getting anxious. It was the first meeting of our new church plant. About fifty adults and twenty children from a nearby church were meeting together for the first time on a Sunday morning. All our plans were laid but we weren't sure how it was going to go, and right now the caretaker wasn't helping! He soon arrived and it turned into one of the best mornings I remember.

Everyone was excited. Everyone arrived early (well, almost everyone). Everyone was pleased to be there. Everyone wanted to help. Everyone was conscious that with God's help we were forming something new – something that we trusted God would use for our good and His glory. Over lunch later that day someone smiled and said, 'It was everything we'd hoped it would be'.

Of course that happy morning only came after many months of praying, discussing and planning. Along the way there were a couple of moments when it seemed like it wasn't going to happen; the journey wasn't always easy. And that morning was now over four years ago and some of the shine has been lost: no one arrives early anymore, it's not always easy getting people to help, and some people have decided that the new church is not everything they hoped it would be. Living together as a church over the long term is always going to be harder than starting something new. And yet we trust God has worked in us and through us, that His church has grown and glory has come to Him as a result.

This short book is designed to explore the main issues involved in planting a new church. We'll look at why we should consider planting and different models of church plants. We'll think about the principles that should guide such a move and the practicalities involved. I write as someone passionate about church planting and having had some experience of it – but not as the 'expert'!

My simple hope is that this will aid anyone and any church wanting to think about planting a new church. Some may decide to try to plant as a result and I pray they'll see the joy of a new church growing. Others may decide not to, but

I hope they'll see the ongoing growth of their current church. Some of course may try to plant but then see it fold — we need to say that that does happen. But even then I pray that valuable lessons will have been learnt and that the church will still grow.

It is, after all, about the growth of the church. The Lord Jesus said:

> I will build my church, and the gates of death will not overcome it. (Matt. 16:18)

Our desire and aim is that Jesus uses us in His plan of building His church.

1

Reasons for planting a church

I once sat in a church meeting discussion about whether or not we should try to plant a new church. Someone stood up and argued strongly that we should go ahead: 'It's Biblical', he said, 'God tells us to do it in His word, and we'd be disobeying if we don't.' No arguing with that then! Except people do. The speaker in that meeting wasn't quite right as there is no actual command to 'Go and plant churches'; rather the command in the Great Commission is to 'Go and make disciples' (Matt. 28:19-20). And so there is debate as to what exactly the Bible says about church planting and whether churches can plant if they happen to feel like it, or whether they should plant.

THE EXAMPLE OF CHURCH PLANTING
The missionary journeys of Paul and his companions (in Acts 13 onwards) clearly resulted

in churches being formed. In Acts 14:21-23 Paul and Barnabas perform the return leg of the first missionary journey and go back to the believers in the towns they've visited, and we read this:

> Paul and Barnabas appointed elders for them in each church and, with prayer and fasting, committed them to the Lord, in whom they had put their trust. (Acts 14:23)

So here are new groups of believers being referred to as individual 'churches' and having leaders appointed. The task of evangelisation (spreading the message of the gospel) and seeing people converted doesn't result in individual believers but the gathering of those believers into new churches. The fulfilment of the great commission in whichever country we live, and around the world, should therefore be tied directly to the formation of new churches. Spreading the gospel message should result in churches being planted.

This means we can immediately agree on some situations in which church planting should take place – that is in an area which has no gospel witness. This is seen most clearly in a classic overseas mission situation where there is no church in a locality. We would want a mission team to speak the gospel, see people come to faith and create a new church. But the same can be seen in our countries that have significant churches already, such as the UK or the USA – there are villages, towns and significant parts of cities with no faithful gospel witness. Sending teams of people to reach these areas is something we should all want to see, and that will involve church planting.

There are some pragmatic questions over this, most specifically: how far away does a locality have to be from an existing church before we should try to plant there? In many cases of course this isn't simply a question of distance but social dynamics. We need to ask: would anyone from that area ever come to this church? Does anyone in this church have contact with people from that area? Despite the questions the point is clear: churches should consider whether they can give themselves to growth of the kingdom by church planting in 'new' parts of their town or city or into a nearby village.

But perhaps the biggest question over church planting is what churches should do about growing in their 'own patch'. Should churches simply get bigger, with bigger buildings or with multiple services – or should they look to plant? This leads us to the issue of church growth.

THE ISSUE OF CHURCH GROWTH

We've said there is no command for individual churches to plant new churches. Rather, as we read of churches forming in Acts and the letters written to such churches, we see that the hope and expectation is that churches will grow. For example Luke summarizes the spread of the gospel by saying:

So the word of God spread. The number of disciples in Jerusalem increased rapidly, and a large number of priests became obedient to the faith. (Acts 6:7)

So the churches were strengthened in the faith and grew daily in number. (Acts 16:5)

As the gospel is spread and people are converted they join the existing church. But that existing church may grow best by planting more churches.

This is what seems to have happened in the first century. Christian meetings were limited to people's homes and so there was a physical limitation on how large a church could become. As the church grew new groups formed in new homes. The church in Jerusalem was something of an exception in that they could meet at the temple – but even then they also met in homes (see Acts 2:42-47). There is then a debate about how these different 'congregations' related to each other, but the point is that they didn't buy or build a bigger building to meet in.

Church planting in the first century was like this at least partly because there was little other option, and so should not be taken to mean that church buildings or large churches are wrong. However it does give us a model of church growth that we have tended to ignore.

LEARNING FROM OBSERVATION
Research into church growth has shown that smaller churches grow faster than larger churches.

Those that are fewer than 100 people in size grow twice as fast proportionally than churches with 100-200 people. And the statistics get worse the bigger the church gets. This would suggest we would be better at reaching our nation if our strategy was planting lots of smaller churches rather than growing fewer larger ones. We need to be careful in reading such statistics as numerous factors can be at work here other than size; however we should not be blind to such observations.

New ways of reaching people

Church plants also provide new opportunities in reaching people with the gospel. They usually have a blank sheet of paper in terms of what they do and how they organize themselves. They can be missionally focused from day one. They have great flexibility, fewer inhibitions, and can often take risks in a way that an established church normally wouldn't. All this means that planting a church may well be the best way to stimulate evangelism whether your church building is full or not.

Thinking about a healthy church

There is also the question as to how size plays into the healthy functioning of church. Larger churches can easily have more people as 'passengers', have less ownership of the mission of the church, and less living out of gospel community. That is not to say large churches are necessarily bad at these things – they will simply have to work harder at them. However, it is to say that we mustn't believe the myth that 'bigger is better' in the world of churches – a myth that always stifles church planting.

WHEN IS A CHURCH A CHURCH?

Another issue to consider in church planting is: what makes a church a church? The reason to ask this question is that how we answer it profoundly influences what we think church planting involves. Are we trying to produce a 'clone' of the church we are currently in or can we plant something that looks quite different?

The churches of the first century are identifiable as a group of people who meet together. Hence Paul writes to the Christians who meet together in Philippi or Corinth (e.g. Phil. 1:1; 1 Cor. 1:2). So a church plant is clearly more than an occasional or *ad hoc* gathering of Christians; rather it is a group which is committed to each other as a church. A church should also soon have an established leadership – see for example Acts 14:23 and Titus 1:5.

But apart from these factors, a church is known much more for its *functions* than its *form*. Functions like teaching, encouraging, loving, caring, praying, praising and spreading the gospel. When Luke wants to describe what the church is about in Acts he says:

> They devoted themselves to the apostles' teaching and to fellowship, to the breaking of

bread and to prayer. Everyone was filled with awe at the many wonders and signs performed by the apostles. All the believers were together and had everything in common. They sold property and possessions to give to anyone who had need. Every day they continued to meet together in the temple courts. They broke bread in their homes and ate together with glad and sincere hearts, praising God and enjoying the favour of all the people. And the Lord added to their number daily those who were being saved. (Acts 2:42-47)

Hence when thinking about church planting we must not necessarily think of replicating what we know of as a church – including a building, a full time minister, a music group, printed bulletins, youth groups and so on. Rather we can think very flexibly of any group committed to praying, learning, and growing together. This flexibility goes hand in hand with the size of a church: in the New Testament a small group meeting together in a house was a perfectly healthy church whereas today we easily think suspiciously of such a structure.

THE KEY QUESTION

The key question for any church to consider is simply this: how can we best grow both in quality of discipleship and spread of the gospel? The answer might mean staying as one church. It might mean planting another. It might mean planting many!

SUMMARY

There are two questions for a church to consider:

1. Can we plant a church in a new area that we currently do not reach to see the spread of the gospel there?

2. How can we best see gospel growth in our current area – is it through growing a larger church, or planting new churches?

2

Different models of church planting

There are numerous models of how to go about church planting. This section will give a brief overview of the main models around today. Be aware that there is some overlap between these different classifications. The second part of this book contains case studies which give a variety of real life examples of these different models.

1. START UP CHURCH

This is the formation of a new church in an area 'from scratch'. This might be into a new town or village; it might be into a new area of a city. As this is planting into new territory this often involves a core group of people moving into the designated area specifically to start the new church. However it can be that there are people already living in that area but currently travelling out of it to different churches.

Where people need to move into the target area, this model clearly demands a high degree of commitment as it requires moving house, children moving school and often moving jobs. One result of this is that a long time is typically spent in building a core team. That team will meet to pray and develop their vision for the church and plan how and when it will start. Then once plans are laid they will each begin to move into the area in question. If enough people are already resident in the target area then it usually requires a reasonable amount of time networking with them and the churches they are currently involved with.

Sometimes this type of plant is part of a collaboration of a network of churches. So the core team may be built from people in different parts of the country but they are all part of the same church network. That is how they hear of the possibility of the new church starting, and the network oversees the plant. It might provide accountability for the leadership and may provide funding in the initial stages.

2. MOTHER-DAUGHTER

This is where a church in one part of a town or city starts a new church relatively nearby. It is a way of growing the church within an area, or 'migrating' into a nearby area. A plant might be started because the mother church simply cannot grow anymore within the physical restraints of its building. Or the plant might be aimed at reaching a group or area that the current church is not reaching. Or it might be that there is a principled decision for one church not to grow too large which results in a decision to plant once the mother church is at a certain size.

Often a group from within the mother church is selected, or volunteers themselves,d they start meeting in the chosen area. Often leadership is provided by some from the mother church leadership moving to be with the plant. The two churches may be very closely connected for a while until the daughter church grows. For example they may share an evening service, have a joint leadership team, or share finances.

3. ON-SITE PLANT

One of the most common tactics used when a church is growing and becoming too large for its meeting space is to have multiple services. Sometimes these are a 'repeat' of each other – so you can choose whether to go to a 9.30am or 11.00am service but they will be identical. Alternatively these may be quite different and aimed at different groups of people, for example a 9.30am families service or a 7.00pm youth service.

Starting a new service is often not thought of as planting a new church – and rightly so because people move back and forth between the different meetings and there is the same leadership over them all. However it is perfectly possible (and some would say preferable) to think in terms of an on-site plant. This is where the new service, although meeting in the same building, has a distinct identity. In this way it is almost identical to the mother-daughter model, the only difference is that the daughter meets in the same place as the mother church.

This means that the congregation must understand that this is not an alternative service but a new church. Movement between the new and old congregations is therefore discouraged. Differences from a simple additional service include: a distinct leadership, separate small groups, separate outreach events, independent finance, and the new church being known by a different name. There may of course be some shared ministries between the two churches but they are distinct entities. One disadvantage of this model is that explanation of the arrangement can be easily misunderstood as being an alternative service. However it can provide a very straightforward way to grow within one area of a city or town.

4. HOUSE CHURCH

House churches are by their nature much smaller in size – they need to fit into someone's house! House church plants are often formed by one house church growing and then deciding to split into two. In that way it can be a much smaller version of the mother-daughter model above. Alternatively a house church plant can be formed by gathering a core group from different churches, or from one larger church. That might be to specifically start a different style of church, or to reach a specific group of people or to reach a specific area of a city (and so a house church can be one way that the 'start up model' above is achieved).

The small size and different ethos of a house church makes some of the practicalities of church planting quite different to the models but the principles involved remain the same.

5. MULTI-SITE CHURCH

A multi-site church has a number of congregations meeting in different locations but which remain united as one church structure. Typically there will be an overall leadership structure, but with local leadership for each congregation. There is often shared finance. Starting a new church plant is often similar to the mother-daughter model above – what is different is that what is aimed at is not an independent church but another congregation as part of the overall church. That difference affects a number of the practicalities of planting.

6. NETWORK COLLABORATION

Some churches are part of a network of churches across the country or in a specific city or area. Being part of such a network can result in a different model of church planting, as leadership and members of the core team can be drawn from different churches in the network. This was mentioned above as one of the ways a 'start up' type plant could be formed. But network collaboration can work in different ways. For example a networked group of churches in a city may collaborate to plant a new church in the same city and provide funding and oversight. This style is a sort of mixture between the mother-daughter model and the multi-site model.

7. RE-START CHURCH

This is where a group of people move to an existing church to 're-start' or reinvigorate it. This model is very different to the others in that it means there are two groups of people who form the new church – those who were part of the original church and those who arrive from elsewhere. The new group could be from a larger local church and so it is a little like the mother-daughter arrangement.

This model has great benefits in revitalising an existing church but also raises a host of issues that are not faced in the other models. In all the models above the planting group along with their mother church or network can decide what the plant will look like, what its vision and practice will be and so on. In this model the new group and the existing church have to work together to decide what the future will look like. There usually has to be a great deal of openness on the part of the existing church to new ways of doing things, rather than simply perpetuating their current style of church but with the presence of new people.

SUMMARY

There are clearly many different ways of going about church planting. Some of these will instinctively appeal to some people because they like the idea or perhaps have seen that model work well elsewhere. Others will react against certain models. What we need to do now is think through how you decide which model you might pick and why.

3

Deciding on a model

We've outlined the main models used in church planting. Now we need to think through which model might be for us.

A FORMULA FOR PICKING A MODEL

Here is a 'formula' for choosing a church planting model. There are three factors which add together to give the model you will choose.

We'll think through each element in the formula and how they add together.

1. Beliefs about church

God teaches us in His word how we should live together as church (what is called 'ecclesiology' in the systematic theology books). We are not free to make up the principles of church life as we wish! And so our beliefs about church from Scripture will influence the model of plant we might choose.

For example:

- some would argue against a multi-site church because they believe that local churches ought to be independent with local leadership only; meanwhile others will think that Biblical principles of church allow for multi-site churches or various forms of networks.

- some believe that the community nature of church life means that a house church is the best way to grow; meanwhile others will think that the principles of community can be worked out in a larger church.

- some believe that churches should be very mixed in their make up: age, background, ethnicity, etc, and so will only organize a plant that is open to everyone; meanwhile others think it's permissible to focus a church on one group such as young professionals, and hence might meet in the evenings (and so exclude families).

We need to be honest that we will have different convictions about church. We also need to see that these are and indeed should be a major factor in the model of plant we choose. My aim here is not to argue for a specific position; rather my concern is to encourage people to think through the beliefs about church that should affect planting, rather than being attracted to certain models for more superficial reasons. *What we think church is guides what sort of church we want to plant.*

2. Aim and purpose

The specific aim and purpose of the plant will also affect the model chosen. For example if the mother church is currently too large to grow in its building, the main aim may be to plant so as to allow ongoing growth in the same locality both in a plant and in the mother church. This will lend itself to the mother-daughter arrangement where a reasonable number of people leave and create space in the mother church as well as forming a new congregation.

By contrast if the aim is to reach a specific group of people, for example those living on a specific housing estate or to focus on ministry to refugees, then it might be preferable to have a relatively small number involved. This will then leave the mother church much the same size.

There will of course be an overlap with our beliefs about church here. Suppose we think that church should be very locally focused and so people should live in the locality rather than travel some distance to church meetings. This will mean that the aim for a plant is to grow a new church focused on a new locality and will result in a plant being narrowed to those who live in that new locality for the plant, or those who are willing to move there.

3. Context

While there are similarities between many churches and planting situations there are always some differences in each context, for example the context of the area of the church and where the plant might be. This will include the geography of the locality – would people consider going to a church that meets on the other side of a main road? It also includes the social dynamics of the local community – which areas use which schools, or whether an area has a close knit social dynamic or is very diffused. One of the models above was the 're-start' church – whether that is even a possibility is totally determined by your context, is there such a church nearby and are they interested in such a venture?

There is also the context of the church (or network) that is planting. Some may be more traditional in their view of church and find some models too daunting; whereas other churches would happily try doing things very differently. There will be differences in the number of people available to plant and the gifts and skills they will contribute. These issues can mean that while we might ideally choose one model of planting, in reality we have to choose another.

Given that none of us are in an ideal context, church leaders will have to make decisions about what the appropriate model is, given *their* context. It is important here not to simply compare with how someone else has done it elsewhere – that may or may not be repeatable in your context.

SUMMARY

There are a number of factors that play into which model of plant is chosen. There is a great deal of flexibility here and our context plays a large part, but there are also principled decisions that flow from our beliefs about church.

Questions:

1. What foundational beliefs about the nature of church will affect the sort of plant you would consider?

2. What specific aims do you have in planting a church? What effect do they have on the model of plant you might choose?

3. Is there anything in your context (your area or your church) that will influence the model you might choose?

4

Different methods of church planting

Consider these stories:

- One church announced to its congregation one day that there would be a church plant starting; the congregation knew that planting was part of the ethos of the church but weren't involved in deciding on when a new plant might happen. The leadership had decided on the date, the location and the leader of the new church. The congregation were asked to consider whether they would like to be part of this new work.

- A church began a discussion in a church members' meeting as to whether they should think about planting. The discussion was inconclusive and was followed by prayer meetings and more discussion in several members' meetings. Eventually a decision was taken to press ahead and a series of meetings was organized for those who might be interested in joining the plant to find out more and help shape what it might look like. This group met many times before the plant started, discussing their priorities as a church and praying together.

- Two families met together and plotted a church plant. They outlined what its aims would be and what it would look like. They discussed who they knew that they might invite to consider joining, and began to talk to churches in the area they wanted to plant into.

- A home group began to develop a vision for the local area in which they met. They prayed specifically for contacts in the area and saw some progress in this. A few in the group began to think about starting a new church in this area based on the current home group. They spoke to their church leadership about this and eventually the home group was 'sent' by the church as a plant.

Having decided on the model of church plant you are interested in there are very different methods of *how* you might go about planting it. In this section we will outline the factors that affect our method as well as our model. We will go into greater detail on some of the 'how' in the next section.

FACTORS IN PICKING A METHOD

1. Model chosen

The method is clearly affected by the model of plant that is to be formed. A start up plant will be created in a very different way to a mother-daughter plant (the third example above was a start up plant – which in the end never happened). A house church is typically quite small and the group is often formed through discussions and working out a plan together, rather than an open invitation to whoever wants to join. The last example above began as a house church whereas the first two examples were mother-daughter plants and so invited people from across the church.

2. Beliefs about church

This specifically includes your beliefs about leadership and decision making in the local church or across a network. Some churches are 'congregational' in decision making and that will be reflected in their method of deciding if and where to do a church plant. That is clearly seen in the second example above.

Perhaps more subtle is the belief about what degree of involvement people should have in shaping a plant and how they relate to the leadership. This is seen in the later stages of the second example as opposed to the first example. Similarly if there is strong ethos of church as 'family' then the method chosen will look quite different to a 'top-down' leadership model.

3. Aim and purpose

If the aim is to move a reasonably large number of people out of a current church to start a new plant then you won't hand pick a few people – rather the process will be designed to include as many people as possible. Conversely if the aim is to reach a targeted group of people e.g. refugees, then you will clearly design a process that only draws in people who want to be involved in achieving that vision.

4. Context

Different churches simply have different ways of doing things – that might be represented in the ways formal decisions are made e.g. by voting or never voting. In addition there will be church councils or elderships, church wardens or deacons and church meetings of different types. This context profoundly affects the method of a plant.

The current situation in the mother church also affects the method. The first example above had an established ethos of church planting such that the congregation was not surprised by the announcement of a plant. Whereas in the second example there was a very mixed reaction and the congregation had to be won round – that meant the whole process took longer. The fourth example had a group that was interested in planting who had formed naturally within the church whereas elsewhere such a group needs to be formed. All these different contextual factors play in the method chosen.

SUMMARY

The main point of this discussion is to show that there is great flexibility in how a plant is formed and so to expect variation between churches and situations. However this flexibility is again to be driven by the principles and beliefs about what church is. *What we think church is affects not only the type of church we want to plant but also how we go about planting it.*

QUESTIONS

1. Consider how your method of church planting will be influenced by:

   • your preferred model of plant.

   • your foundational beliefs about church.

   • the aim and purpose of the plant.

   • your current context (include decision making; involvement in networks; the current ethos of the church, etc).

5

Key issues in church planting

Having discussed some of the variety of models and methods of planting we will now focus on some of the key issues faced in the method chosen.

FORMING A CORE GROUP

All church plants involve developing a core group which will form the church. The size of this group will depend on the model of plant chosen and the planting context (e.g. the size of the mother church). There are also very different ways of choosing who is in this core group.

Hand-picked team

One approach is the hand-picked team. This is where the leadership of the mother church, the network, or the new plant (or some combination) hand-pick people and invite them to form the core group. The invitation usually includes careful outlining of what the plant will involve and what is expected of them. Hence the bar for being included is usually raised very high.

This has the advantage of only including those in the core group who are trusted and known. There is usually a high degree of commitment to the aim of the plant – everyone is very much 'on side' with what the plant is trying to do. This approach usually goes hand in hand with a smaller team however and so is common for house churches. A disadvantage is that if operating within a mother church the plant can appear to be an 'elite' group.

Open door

At the other end of the spectrum is an 'open door' approach. That is to have the core group open to anyone who is interested – here the bar for entry is very low. This might well be called the 'revolving door' approach as well, because it often involves people both coming into and leaving the core group if they decide it's not for them.

The disadvantage of this approach is that you could end up with a very disparate group of people with very different ideas of what they want the plant to be. This can be addressed however, and is discussed in the next point. Another disadvantage is that the leadership will not immediately know who is actually committed to the plant. This ignorance can be avoided by good communication such that the leaders know who is definitely committed, who is probable and who is unlikely.

The advantage of this approach is that you can include a large number of people very easily, and so it is most common for a mother-daughter model. It can also mean the plant has a 'come and see' feel to it. People know they can find out more and see what it might be like without having to immediately 'sign up'. One result can be people being included who wouldn't have done so had the bar been set high at the start.

Mixed approaches

You can of course have a mixture of these approaches. For example you can have an open door for whoever is interested in coming, but then also specifically invite certain people to come because you want them to play a key role within the plant. You can also have an open door policy but with some kind of informal 'interview' to make sure people know what they are committing to and asking why they want to be part of the plant.

In a mother-daughter model the creation of the core group presents a challenge to the attitudes of the leadership. It can easily become a tug of war over the people considered most valuable in the church, with one group arguing they should be invited on the plant and others that they should stay! This is where there needs to be both good communication and godly attitudes. We want to see a growing plant and a revitalized mother church and so the health of both congregations needs to be in everyone's minds. In addition, the actual process of who decides whom to invite needs to be clear to everyone. Leadership teams can benefit from some honest discussion over these issues before the process actually starts.

Managing the core group

If an open door policy is adopted then one issue is managing whom exactly goes. It could be, for example, that too many people are interested and it would cripple the mother church. Or it can be that too few are interested for the model of plant envisaged. Or perhaps all of the people in their twenties and early thirties are planning on going which will rob the mother church of a generation. Or perhaps most of the Sunday school teachers or music group are interested – or conversely none of them are.

These issues mean that with an open door policy the leadership needs to manage the core group. In practice this means explaining what is happening to the whole church and often asking some to consider going or staying.

Identifying reasons for going (and staying)

The reasons people decide to go on a plant (or not go) can be summed up with five 'P's.

• Project

Some people love the whole idea of a plant or the specific aims of this plant and so the project itself is what attracts them. They don't mind where it is or who's leading it, they just want to be part of it.

• Person leading

The person (or people) leading the new plant will be a factor for many. They will like or dislike that person's style of teaching or leading (or just not like them as a person!).

• Place

The place that the plant is going to meet will affect many people. They might live down the road and so not think they have much choice; or they might live across town and so rule it out.

• People going

Perhaps one of the biggest factors can be who else is going on the plant. This is where you can get 'clumping' of groups. Once people discover that a critical mass of their friends is interested they then decide to go as well. But equally if a few key people are not going then they choose to stay.

• 'Put out'

Some people are unhappy in a church – they are 'put out' in some way. Maybe they feel on the edge of things, maybe they feel disillusioned, maybe they've fallen out with someone or maybe they take exception with the way things are done. These may or may not be bad attitudes, but they can all mean someone decides to join a plant simply because it is somewhere other than the current church.

It is part of the role of the leadership to help people make good decisions for good reasons. We want to see servant-heartedness such that people are willing to be wherever would be most helpful for the gospel. But there will need to be leadership and teaching if that is to happen. There will also need to be many conversations with individuals to help them decide whether to go or stay.

LEADERSHIP PROCESS

In forming the plant there needs to be a process that decides what the plant will look like. For example: what its main aims and mission will be; what 'feel' will it have; how will teaching be done; what will be the role of small groups; how will evangelism happen; etc.

'Blueprint'

One approach is for the leadership of the plant (perhaps in conjunction with the mother church or network if there is one) to answer these questions. They formulate a 'blueprint' of what the plant will look like. This means of course that the leadership hold the process in their own hands and people joining can't disrupt what is hopefully a clear vision.

In addition this approach means that people who are interested in the plant know exactly what they are getting into, which helps them in their decision as to whether to be part of the plant or not. The downside of this is that there is very little ownership of the vision of the plant.

Consultation

A different approach is to have a much more consultative process. Here those who are interested in joining can actually contribute to shaping the plant. The ownership is usually then very high – often with a concomitant degree of commitment.

The disadvantage is that you could get lots of very different and sometimes incompatible ideas being fed in. Also the leadership will presumably have some ideas of their own and would want to see them implemented.

Halfway house

There is of course a halfway house approach where the leadership put certain elements in place and then allow discussion and consultation on exactly how some things get worked out. It is important that this is a genuine process however, such that the end result might not look exactly as the leaders might have thought. Exactly how such consultation takes place will depend on the model of plant being adopted and the maturity of those involved.

VISION & STRATEGY

Linked with the question of leadership process above is what the eventual vision and strategy of the plant church looks like.

Replication

It is not uncommon in mother-daughter plants for the daughter church to aim at being a replica of the mother. This is often quite a positive sign in that those planting have a high view of the mother church and aren't leaving in order to change things! There is the advantage that everyone knows what they are aiming at together.

The disadvantage is that the opportunity to think through new ways of doing things is not taken. Whether this is an issue depends greatly on the health of the mother church and how appropriate the strategy is there. A replication approach can also mean that planting is only considered if a reasonable replica can be formed – which can mean not planting when a different model of plant would have been perfectly possible.

'Blank sheet of paper'

At the other end of the spectrum is to have a 'blank sheet of paper' approach where the vision and strategy of the plant is completely open. It might be open for the new plant leadership to decide or for the core group to help shape depending on the approach taken on leadership process.

The great advantage of this is that new ideas and ways of doing things can be considered. Even if the plant ends up looking similar to the mother church the process of thinking through why we do what we do in the way we do it is usually very valuable. And any differences in the plant show its adaption to those in it and to those they are trying to reach. Disadvantages can be: a plant group overreacting against the mother-church's way of doing things; spending time reinventing the wheel; trying to be different for the sake of it.

New ways of doing old things

One way of thinking about developing the vision and strategy of a plant is that it is looking for new applications of old principles. So for example, teaching from God's word will take place – but the plant can consider new ways this can be done more helpfully, or what would be the most strategic way of teaching given the group they are trying to reach. Similarly evangelistic strategies or events can be thought through in the new context and with the specific aims of the plant.

The plant may have a very different structure and specific aims compared to a mother church and so look very different in practice; or it may look relatively similar. However the process of thinking through together how this group will live out the biblical principles of church is one of the great advantages and blessings of a church plant.

Constitutional issues

A plant doesn't need a constitution! To think it does is to buy into our current models of church as the only way to do things. However, a church plant does need to decide how it will operate

– for example how leadership will function or how decisions will be made. This is the stuff of constitutions which are best thought of as the 'house-rules' of the family.

So whether they are written down and printed out as a constitution or are simply known and accepted they do need to be thought through. These include:

- Leadership: is there a single appointed leader? If so, who are they accountable to and how are they appointed? Is there an eldership or a church council of some kind? If so who is eligible to be on it and how will they be chosen?

- Decision making: how will decisions be made as a church? In a house church that might be as simple as saying, 'We'll just talk it through'. In a larger plant there probably needs to be a clearer process distinguishing what lies in the hands of the leaders and what the congregation has a say in (for example by discussion or voting).

- Doctrinal distinctives: what will the church's position be on baptism, charismatic gifts or the role of women in the life of the church?

It's important to say that these issues are not the heart of planting a church! Many of them can be accepted as read in most situations and many can be left until the point in the life of the church when it becomes necessary to discuss them. So don't think you need a gold-plated constitution before you can plant. And be aware that constitutions don't make for well run, happy, united churches – that's all about godliness and good relationships.

CHOOSING AN AREA

How important the selection of the area to plant is depends on the model of church planting you are using. Some churches aim to be networks of friendships and contacts rather than being centred on a locality, and so where they happen to meet is less important. Sometimes the locality will have been effectively chosen already – because it is a re-start plant, or it is a house church growing out of an existing home group, or because the plant is starting specifically to focus on a new area.

Other times there will be free reign as to where a plant might start. A major issue here has to be where other churches are in the city or town. This will inevitably involve a judgement as to whether these are gospel-preaching and Bible-teaching churches and respectful contact with other churches is appropriate.

If the plant is coming from a mother church one helpful technique can be to use a map plot of where everyone currently lives and to include on that other evangelical churches. That process can reveal an obvious area where some people are already living and where there is no local church – although by itself this doesn't decide the issue.

There can sometimes be nervousness about stepping into another church's 'patch'. We should be respectful and communicate well, but we must also remember that there are so many people around who need to hear the gospel we are very unlikely to cramp each other's style.

RELATIONSHIP WITH 'MOTHER-SHIP'

In a mother-daughter plant there needs to be thought given as to how the relationship between the two churches will work. We can see the options by considering two extremes.

Wave goodbye at the door

One route is to launch the plant as an independent entity from day one. The 'cut' from the mother church is complete from the start and so there is no ongoing relationship – other than communication of news, prayer and informal connections.

This means the church plant has to plan and organize what it will do about various ministry areas such as small groups, youth work, Sunday meetings and so on, before it launches. Of course as we have said already there is no need for the plant to try to do all that the mother church might have done and so a plant can launch with a much reduced ministry load.

One key area that does need to be decided on is leadership, as the church will be independent of the leadership of the mother church. Finance will also need to be thought through as to whether the plant can be self-sustaining from the start.

The advantage of this approach is that the plant is its own entity from the start. It can begin with a clean slate in all areas and so develop its own ethos and vision clearly. How much of an issue this is of course depends on how distinct the plant is from the mother church.

Home every weekend

At the other end of the spectrum the plant starts a new meeting but still 'comes home' regularly. So for example a Sunday morning meeting might begin but then there is a joint Sunday evening service such that the plant group comes back to the mother church each Sunday night. Mid-week meetings, small groups, youth groups and so on can all remain the same.

The advantage of this method is ease – all you have to organize is a Sunday morning meeting (or whatever gathering you have decided on). The leadership of the mother church can retain oversight and finance need not be an issue. For churches who are concerned about the plant not succeeding, this route can be more reassuring. The main disadvantage is that the plant is an addition to the mother church, not an entity in its own right.

You can of course begin with this strategy but plan to separate elements of church life over the following months. If this 'stepped' departure is planned it is crucial that everyone knows what the eventual aim is – otherwise what began as a mother-daughter church plant can become a multi-site church by default.

It is of course possible to continue areas of shared ministry with the mother church (this is most common in networks of churches but happens elsewhere as well). For example training events, mid-week youth work, or annual events of various kinds might all continue as a shared ministry between the two churches. Clear communication and clear lines of oversight are essential.

Legal issues

Depending on what model of church plant you have decided on and whether you are part of a larger denomination, you may or may not have to worry about legalities. However many new churches will have to register themselves as charities so as to be able to run their finances on a charitable basis. One advantage of not leaving the mother-church too fully at the start is that finances can be run through that church. However these issues may need to be faced at some point and there are several organisations that can help advise and even administer some of this for you (see the resources and further reading section).

YOUTH AND CHILDREN'S MINISTRY

One of the most common concerns with church planting is the effect it will have on children's and youth ministry. In a mother-daughter plant people in the mother church can be concerned about a weakening of their children's ministry; and those in the plant group concerned about what provision there will be for their children. This later concern about provision for children in the plant is true of virtually every model of plant because of the smaller numbers often involved.

It is important to remind ourselves here of the prime responsibility of parents in teaching and training their children – sometimes these concerns are expressed because parents have effectively handed over responsibility for this to the church. But having said that, there are often reasonable questions to be asked.

In a mother church it is usually an issue of finding new people to help teach and lead groups to take the place of those who are leaving for the plant. This is often needed in other areas of service in the church as well. This can actually be one of the beneficial effects for the mother church of planting – it stimulates more people to get involved and serve. In larger well-established churches this is usually a very positive thing, but can still feel daunting. The leadership will need to guide the church in this and give appropriate reassurances.

In a plant church the most common issue is the small number of children, resulting in wide age-ranges in a Sunday school class or a lack of peers for some children. This can of course make a plant seem unattractive to a child and hence their family. Once again, though, we must say there are more ways of teaching our children than a traditional Sunday school set-up.

For example, with smaller numbers an older child might help teach younger ones, maybe having prepared with an adult (and may learn far more in the process); some children could help with practical tasks e.g. crèche, and then have a teaching slot with an older person elsewhere in the week. Having groups with a wide age-range makes teaching more difficult but introduces the dynamics of love and patience to the children. One advantage in a plant is that children tend to feel much more part of the church and get to know people other than their peers. Shared mid-week youth ministries, if available, can provide opportunity for further peer friendships.

STAFFING / LEADERSHIP

A common question about church plants is whether you need a full time staff member (usually a pastor) for it to happen. The answer of course is 'No'; there is no *need* for a pastor. What there is, is a need for leadership, teaching and pastoral oversight. The key question is whether or not those things are in place, rather than assuming they need to be delivered through a paid staff member.

This clearly relates to the model of plant chosen and the numbers involved. A house church is unlikely to be able to support a full-time member of staff (and wouldn't need to). A larger more traditionally organized church doesn't necessarily need such a person but may function better with one in place. For mother-daughter plants one very common approach is for the mother church to employ an assistant pastor with a view to their leading a church plant. A network plant often designates a staff member to lead it as well.

In considering leadership, it's worth pointing out that the skill set and character of a church planter is often said to differ from the average church minister. It is said that they should be a risk taker, an evangelist, prepared to work with scarce resources and have a 'can do' attitude. There is some truth to this as the church plant context does raise challenges. Exactly what gifts and character are needed though depends greatly on the model of plant used. Some plants are more challenging pioneering situations; others are starting a new congregation of a large well-established church. What will clearly be needed is the ability to lead a group in a new venture, and so leadership gifting is clearly needed. Exactly what other gifts should be present will depend on the context and the mix of other leaders involved.

6

The early days
of planting

VARIETY OF EXPERIENCES

It is worth being clear from the start – every church plant is different! Church plants come from different churches; they are based on different models; they are planted into different contexts; they may have different aims; they have different leaders; and they are made up of different people. As a result every plant is different and we should beware of thinking that someone else's experience will be our own.

It is particularly important for churches not to look at what another church has done and then presume that exactly the same results will happen if they follow the same model. There are usually many lessons to learn from others' situations but these virtually always need 'translating' into your own context.

COMMON FACTORS
Having said there are differences, there are also some common factors in how church plants go.

• Enthusiasm

Most plants begin with great enthusiasm. This assumes the process has resulted in a degree of togetherness and excitement. That enthusiasm is to be enjoyed but not to be taken for more than it is. Normal life will start soon enough. All honeymoons come to an end and so will this. The leadership will need to help people see how short-term enthusiasm for something new is turned into long term commitment to something meaningful. The quality of a new church is not shown by the enjoyment of the first months, but the perseverance needed when it gets harder.

• Disappointment

There can be disappointment as a plant starts – perhaps the process of planting has been fraught or even acrimonious and it begins with a bad taste in the mouth. If so the leadership will need to lead people to respond appropriately.

There can be individual disappointment – perhaps close friends decided not to come having said they would and so some people are wondering if they want to be there. For many, disappointment can appear as they realize the plant isn't going to be exactly what they hoped. This might be because of a particular agenda they had; or it could be that they had unrealistic expectations.

• Baggage

Some people will bring particular baggage with them. The person who's come to escape a relationship at the old church; the person with a chip on their shoulder or who is nursing a grievance; the person who'd like a new chance to use their gifts; the person who was let down by previous church leaders.

Of course all of us in churches have baggage of different types. The point is that the early days of a church plant can often be times when it is revealed and the leadership will need to be alert and ready to handle this. And this can be embraced positively – handled well this can be a great time of growth for that person.

• New people

The great hope is that new people will come to the plant. The really great hope is that they will be people being converted. The plant will need to be thoughtful and ready for how such people will be integrated and taught. However, there may be new people who come who are already Christians – they may have moved to the area, they may have been at other churches nearby and want to change, or they may have drifted from church and see the plant as a fresh start.

The leadership will need to think through what to do with such people. Are they simply welcomed? If they are from another church it is worth asking why they have come. If they've drifted from church its worth asking why that happened. And for all of them it's worth thinking how they will integrate and 'buy into' the vision of the plant. There is a danger that the focus and vision of a plant is diluted by new people joining simply because they heard of something new happening and fancied a change.

SHAPING THE PLANT

There is often a process of shaping the plant in the early days. As you start functioning you can think through how you do all kinds of things from scratch. Some of these will have been decided in your planning before you launched but lots won't have been.

This is where the key aims and vision of the plant are crucial. The ethos, habits and ways of doing things can and should be shaped around those aims and vision. The early days of a plant hold a wonderful opportunity to ask, 'How can we live out what we want to be as church?', or, 'How can we best stand for and achieve our aims?'. Asking those questions allows moulding of church life in both small and large details.

NORMAL LIFE

Church plants don't magically escape normal life. There will be people struggling with sin, sickness, relationships, tragedies, business, family life and so on. A church plant simply gives a new context in which we live out our lives with all their issues together.

Neither does a church plant magically escape some of the normal dynamics of church life. There will be people who aren't confident in speaking about Jesus, who aren't committed to their small group, who struggle to welcome people different to them, who don't like the ways some things are done and so on. A church plant simply gives a new focus to what we want church to be and a new opportunity to engage with it.

The honeymoon period also gradually fades away and a new 'normal life' as a plant emerges. Hopefully it is a normal life with great things about it, but it will be normal life nonetheless with all its challenges, hardships and joys.

CHALLENGES FOR LEADERS

There is always a temptation for Christian leaders to evaluate themselves by how well their ministry is going or what feedback they receive. This is an issue of self-identity and security that every Christian leader needs to be aware of. It is just worth pointing out that the temptations and pressures in this area usually increase with a church plant.

For example, in forming a core group the leader of a plant can feel elated or depressed by the latest news on how many are planning to attend. As the plant starts you can feel flat because no one new has come; or buoyant because of how well it is going.

This is nothing new or different – it is just an intensified version of normal leadership temptations. It's important that leaders are aware of this and care for each other; it's also worth the core group being aware of this and appropriately caring for their leaders.

Conclusion

Our desire is to see God glorified by His gospel being spread and His church growing. This will inevitably mean more churches and so more church planting. That is not to say that every church should be doing a church plant at this moment in time. But surely more churches should be than currently are; and surely every church should hope to be doing so at some point.

There are lots of things to be worked through, and lots of hard work to be done. There will undoubtedly be moments of anxiety and concern. There is the possibility of failure. But there is also the possibility of starting a new group of God's people who grow themselves and see the gospel spread where it wasn't being heard before. There is the potential for real multiplication of gospel ministry.

Many will say that, 'We're not ready', or 'We're not strong enough', or 'It won't work'. Well, there is such a thing as an ill-conceived or poorly planned church plant that is damaging in its effects. But there is also such a thing as a comfortable church that isn't prepared to risk its comfort for the sake of growing the kingdom of God. It is for each church to ask itself – how can we best see the kingdom of God grow, and might that involve planning a church plant?

SECTION 2

Case Studies

The case studies below tell the stories of a number of church plants. They are here to help flesh out the descriptions and principles given so far. They are divided into the different models of planting that were given earlier; however it will be clear that the boundaries between some of these are blurred and some come from very unique contexts. An attempt has been made to give a wide range of types and contexts of planting. Grateful thanks are due to those who've contributed.

1. START UP CHURCH

These are all churches planting into new areas but they vary in where they've come from, the context they've planted into and how they've gone about it. (There are also further examples of start up church that took place as part of a network under the 'Network church' section).

City Church, Birmingham, UK

Three friends (and their families) had lived in Birmingham for some time and had felt there was a clear need for a contemporary evangelical Bible teaching church. We gauged interest by holding three open-house meetings where we set out the vision. Word was spread as friends brought friends and around twenty-five people attended.

Most who came had some connection with an existing church but were looking for a church that was contemporary in style with a deep love for the Lord and the teaching of His word. City Church then began to meet in the front room of the home of one of our elders (with the piano in the back room which made for interesting times when we sang!). Most of those who had attended the open-house meetings then began to come along, and within four or five weeks we were too big for a house.

The eldership of the new church was formed by the three organising members. As City Church was not part of any network or from a mother church, we established a Council of Reference to which the elders were accountable and from which we received advice and guidance.

We began meeting in a local school and this quickly changed the face of the church. Students arrived as did children from the community. Within weeks we were 50-60 on a Sunday. We needed a children's programme, music group and 'set-up' team much more quickly than we had expected but with a clear vision and a united core, church members were far more generous with their time and more enthusiastic to help than we could ever have expected. In the life of a very young church there is little or no room for 'passengers' but everyone was willing to play their part.

—— Neil Powell ——
www.city-church.org.uk

Restoration Church, Washington, DC, USA

I attended Southeastern Baptist Theological Seminary and I took a course by a professor named Dr John Hammett, a man who excels in ecclesiology. Having no deep framework for the local church both Biblically and methodologically, I was amazed as Dr Hammett laid out the glories of Christ revealed and prescribed in the church within the Scriptures.

He recommended going to a 'Weekender' put on by Capitol Hill Baptist Church, incidentally in Washington, DC and there I saw in four days much of what Dr Hammett had taught us. Driving home from that weekend combined with my time in Dr Hammett's class I knew I would either reform or plant a church.

I was very active in my local church through seminary and it was there that I saw the local church in her daily life, warts and all. After a time of doing Biblical community (teaching, leading a small group, serving, evangelizing, etc.), the elders of that church (North Wake Church in Wake Forest, NC) recommended I be a part of their first church-planting residency, and I concurred and took part in that for a year.

After hearing the counsel of the elders combined with my own self-evaluation and prayer I deemed it best to plant rather than reform. This then left the location, which wound up being Washington, DC due to it meeting some qualifications we had prayerfully laid out. Those categories were that the location must be an urban setting which needed a Gospel-centred work that had nations and universities within its confines, all the while being a city of influence and a thinking person's city.

Being committed to a team approach, my family and I moved here with another family. We have lived here now for a year and are still very early in the work. We were supported by my home church as well as being bi-vocational for a while. We are still a very small church, not even a year old, but we have garnered people from every location fathomable. From meeting people on the street, to random connections, to distributing flyers throughout the city and word of mouth. We have started a Sunday morning service but our approach is intentionally quite simple...make disciples by gathering them around the Word inside a Biblical community so that Christ may be made beautiful.

—— Nathan Knight ——

Criccieth Family Church, Criccieth, UK

Criccieth Family Church is unusual in that it came from the local Scripture Union Beach Mission. The Leaders of the Mission live in Criccieth and two mums asked if they could run a Family Service similar to that held during the Beach Mission. We approached our church leader to see if we could run such an alternative service on a Sunday morning, but the answer was 'no' as it would compete with the main service.

We decided to go ahead in the hour before the main service, once a month over an autumn. An encouraging number came and those involved asked to meet more frequently causing us to meet fortnightly. The group consisted of some local families and a number of Christians who had moved into the area and as word got around we also welcomed a number of visitors to this popular holiday area. Five months later we decided to meet weekly.

Several years on, despite the experience of a church split there is both a morning and evening service and a full time pastor.

—— Andrew Bradley ——
www.cricciethfamilychurch.org.uk

The Plant, Manchester, UK

A number of people had noticed there was a woeful lack of Bible-teaching churches in central Manchester, particularly given Manchester's massive student population. God brought seven of us together, including two Anglican curates serving different churches on the edge of Manchester.

It wasn't possible to plant 'from' any one church, but rather we gathered a group of interested people. We initially approached the Diocese of Manchester with our proposal, but the answer was 'not yet'. Nevertheless, we felt compelled to press on and so 'The Plant' (as we creatively called it!) was formed as an independent church.

Throughout this time, we received support from the newly-forming North West Partnership and the Anglican mission agency *Crosslinks*, who took our two Anglican ministers on as Associate Mission Partners. The Plant was launched and within a few years the Bishop of Manchester granted us his 'Permission to Officiate', although we remain independent of Anglican structures.

We were keen to 'strip church down' to the bare, biblical essentials; and concentrating on students and recent graduates gave us exceptional flexibility. From Acts 2:42, we resolved that all our church meetings would incorporate Bible teaching, prayer, discussion time and a meal. We also wanted to do things in such a way that visiting non-Christians would feel most welcome, and be able to see Christ-inspired love in our fellowship (John 13:35). So the model we adopted is one of a number of small congregations (currently three, each about 20 to 30 strong), sharing resources and working together in very close partnership. As we grow, we plant new congregations around the city in appropriate locations (currently a bridge club, a health centre and a pub).

—— Phil Keymer ——
www.theplant.net

Hill City Church, Trevethin Estate, Pontypool, UK
We were commissioned by Highfields Church, Cardiff, to plant a church on Trevethin, a hill top council estate in the South Wales Valleys. Trevethin enjoys a strong sense of community spirit, whilst also facing the challenge of being an area of multiple deprivation.

We felt that the most culturally sensitive approach was to start from scratch. This entailed prayer-walking around the estate for a year, seeking God's timing for the whole mission. We also started to build bridges into the community by providing DJ-ing workshops for local young people.

We bought a house in the heart of the estate and, upon moving in, we started a mid-week home group and were worshipping together as a family each Sunday morning with the conviction that aside from death or divorce, the church could only grow! Right from the beginning the church's vision was missional, so even though we were very few in number, we started to host evangelistic events and to build meaningful relationships with local people. Slowly but surely the church started to grow: initially it was mainly a blend of prodigals and mission-minded Christians who wanted to join the adventure (with the blessing of their church leaders).

After twelve months we couldn't fit in our home so we started (and continue) to meet in the local community centre. Services are very simple: non-flashy sung worship, theologically chunky sermons, good coffee and sincere love. Meeting publicly gave us a much stronger presence in the community and it wasn't long before the locals started popping in to check us out. This coincided with the arrival of two Ministry Apprentices from Highfields who helped us to start several new ministries, including a weekly youth club and a mentoring scheme in the local school. We also got more heavily involved in community projects, launched a men's ministry and started an evangelistic course involving a meal, a gospel talk and coffee-based discussion. During this time we saw our first conversions and held our first baptism service on a beach, complete with barbecue – a fantastic day!

Hill City Church is a beautifully messy church, held together by the glue of grace. Our passion is to see the gospel taking root in Trevethin and beyond, to the glory of Jesus Christ.

—— Dai Hankey ——
www.hillcitychurch.org

Farm Fellowship, Preston, UK

Farm Fellowship was an idea in the mind of one key family for a few years as they worked in a farm shop. This family of five gradually shared their vision with a few others and a weekly Bible study was started on a Sunday morning followed by a communal lunch. There were 12 to 15 people – some were older Christians who shared the vision, but half were new people who wanted to find out more.

At that stage there was very little sense of how it could all develop. The core commitment was to be a group who would work together to put the teaching of Jesus into practice. The focus has always been people who have never been to church. It has now grown to around eighty people including some very close friendships with Muslim families.

The meeting room (a converted barn) is set up with a coffee shop feel, including a cigarette break in the middle of the Sunday meeting. There is always a Bible exposition followed by sharing the needs of the local community and praying about them, co-ordinating who will cook meals, visit, write letters etc. We always eat lunch together and then people hang around for most of the afternoon.

The real life of the Fellowship happens through-out the week, as we apply the teaching of Jesus together where we work and live. We are involved with Christians Against Poverty, Alcoholics Anon-ymous and a homeless project – and throughout the week different members of the Farm Fellow-ship volunteer in these areas. The farm shop helps us to know when people in the area are ill, made redundant, bereaved, struggling – we try to pro-vide meals or support.

—— Paul Blackham ——
www.farmfellowship.com

Christ Church, Liverpool, UK

Christ Church Liverpool was started by a group of about fifteen Christians from half a dozen churches in the Liverpool area who saw the need for a gospel-centred church in the heart of the city. These fifteen people all had some contact with the two leaders of the plant. The vision was to provide a church family for the many Christians who already lived in the city centre and to bring the message of Christ to the thousands of non-Christians who live, work or study there. Because most of the people in the city centre are students and young professionals we tried to shape the church around meeting and sharing the gospel with those groups particularly. The core group met once a month for six months to pray and we divided up specific tasks between us.

When we started, we let people know about the church by word of mouth, through the web and by getting involved in things like Freshers' Fair at the universities. The two leaders were confirmed as suitable elders both by the core group and the churches they were moving from.

Almost all of our evangelism was done through people bringing their friends and family to Christianity Explored and, increasingly over the years, to church on a Sunday morning. We've learned that everything is an experiment and that most of the new things you try won't work. But that's OK – because some of them will.

——Andrew Evans ——
www.christchurchliverpool.org

Harvest Bible Chapel, Glasgow, UK

The typical assessment of church life in Glasgow was that 'there are a few churches that teach God's Word faithfully but often the worship does not allow us to express how excited we are to follow Jesus' or 'there are churches where the music is great but you would not want to stake your future on what was being preached.'

We planned to plant a church under the leadership of Harvest Bible Fellowship (based in Chicago) whose vision is to plant autonomous local churches. They provided training, oversight and the visit of a team from Chicago to help with the launch.

We began the work of planting a church that would be established on four pillars:

- The preaching of the authority of God's Word without apology.

- Lifting high the name of Jesus through (contemporary) worship.

- Believing firmly in the power of prayer.

- Sharing the Good News of Jesus with boldness.

We began meeting people in coffee shops, connecting and re-connecting with relationships via Facebook and held a series of open house information evenings in a local hotel conference suite to share our vision. This resulted in a core group of about twenty people.

The church launched with around 150 people in attendance settling to an average early attendance of anything between 50 and 60 people. Many of those who came to the first meeting were well-wishers or those having an initial look because of publicity. What we have seen is a huge appetite developing in people for God and His Word, a desire to lift Jesus' name high in worship and God doing exactly what we prayed believing that He would – transforming lives.

—— Scott Hamilton ——
www.harvestglasgow.org

2. MOTHER-DAUGHTER

These are all examples of a church seeking to plant a daughter church. However there is huge variation in how it was done, where the new church was planted with respect to the mother church and how the relationship between the two was managed.

Sovereign Grace Church, Middletown, Delaware, USA[1]

Only miles from the Pennsylvania/Delaware border, Covenant Fellowship Church (CFC) in Glen Mills, PA long had a desire to plant a church in the state of Delaware. When I began a church-planting internship in June 2003, the pastoral team asked me to prayerfully consider planting in Delaware. Very quickly, we sensed this was the Lord's will.

---

1. Planted from *Covenant Fellowship Church*, Glen Mills, PA.

After visiting and prayerfully considering several options, we settled on the town of Middletown – a quickly growing semi-rural town, a commuter town of about 13,000 people located near the middle of this small state. Though we considered other higher-populated areas, God gave my wife and me, along with the pastoral team at CFC, a heart to serve, in particular the many families here.

We began making plans for a Fall launch and sought to draw together a church-planting team from CFC. Five couples and three singles responded to the call to join this new venture. In total, the church planting team was made up of fifteen adults. By God's grace, twelve of them remain. Most of the church planting team needed to relocate but most had jobs they were still able to commute to in Northern Delaware.

We recently celebrated our five year anniversary as a church. Our testimony? God has been very good and very faithful! He answered our prayers. A vibrant gospel-centred community of about ninety folks has been established and continues to grow.

The church planting team has more than doubled itself – by filling the creation mandate to 'be fruitful and multiply'! A handful of college students came early on, married, and stayed. Also, a number of Christian families have made this their church home. Some who were travelling outside Middletown to attend church came because they were looking for a church in the town where they lived. We've seen a few conversions as well. All who joined did so because they were drawn to the gospel-centred teaching and fellowship.

Humanly speaking, we haven't had a lot to draw people to Sovereign Grace Church. We don't have the fancy facility; we meet in a school gym. We don't have a lot of programs. We still don't gather a large crowd. However, what we do have is more important than what we don't have. We have the Gospel and the effects of the Gospel.

And the story of Sovereign Grace Church is – it's enough. The Gospel is enough! In fact it's more than enough to birth and establish a local church!

____ Chris Patton ____
www.sovereigngraceministries.org

Hope Community Church, Cambridge, UK[2]
After coming to a consensus that church planting ought to be a key part of our church's evangelism strategy, we began looking at our area more carefully. To avoid unnecessary duplication of gospel effort we set two criteria: *where* do people have least access to a vibrant evangelical church and *which* people are under represented in existing evangelical churches?

We also bore in mind areas where church members were already living. Although the planting team was relatively small we quickly realized that twelve was large compared to many missionary situations much further distant!

---

2. Planted from *Rock Baptist Church*.

We chose a densely populated but quite mixed area with one small evangelical church and two non-evangelical parish churches. We spoke to the pastor of the former to keep him informed, ask his thoughts and assure him we had no designs on his people. There were two main geographical focuses for the area and we decided on two meeting places – an almost disused chapel and a school – since our main means of outreach would be relational rather than people just walking in.

Our emphasis on reaching friends and introducing them to each other has led to film nights, a women's book group (fiction) and joining local clubs. In our Sunday meetings we offer time for discussion and questions and have a meal together afterwards. We've tried to build new relationships through a language café, an over 60s café, gardening help, door-to-door work and a local festival. We're increasingly involved in the local school through regular assemblies, governing and an after-school club.

Our intention from the outset was to avoid growth by transfer: we've rejoiced with a handful who have professed faith and with others moving to the area we've now grown to around thirty.

—Al MacInnes—
www.hopecommunity.org.uk

Christ Church, Brighton, UK[3]

The original idea of Christ Church Brighton came from a member of a church in nearby Hove where

---

3. Planted from *Bishop Hannington Church*, Hove.

I was a curate. He wanted a church in Brighton which he could take friends to. This metamorphosized over some eighteen months into a 'fresh expression of church' supported by the Bishop of Chichester.

The vision put to people was to be committed members of a faithful and contemporary Bible-teaching church which was big on fellowship and big on evangelism. We would work hard at 'being church' together, sharing each others' lives and living out the command to love one another. We would also prioritize the development of relationships with those who are not Christians, seeking to draw them to Christ as we involve them in the life of church members.

The core group was gathered hastily, due in part to the quirks of Anglican Church appointments. I met with individuals and families over a six week period, sharing the vision and asking people to commit for a period of one year. Because of the need to focus on each other and reaching unbelievers, there was a clear expectation that we would be acting like 'missionaries' in another city. Our aim was not just to 'do church' in a different place, but to become a new community, reaching people who had no previous link with church. Only those living in Brighton or who had a network of friends within Brighton (as opposed to Hove) were invited to join. The area in which the church was based was decided by the location of those involved.

The declared aim of not growing through 'transfer growth' has, in the main part, been lived out. Forty-five per cent of the church is unchurched or dechurched. Less than ten per cent of the church has come from another church in Brighton, all with the clear support of their church leadership. Just six of the original fourteen remain – which means that, by God's grace, there are more newly converted people in the church than existing founder members.

—— Carl Chambers ——
www.christchurchbrighton.org

Brandywine Grace Church, Downingtown, PA, USA[4]

For years a core group of believers attending Covenant Fellowship Church in Glen Mills, PA, had been earnestly praying for a Sovereign Grace church plant in Chester County, an area about twenty miles to the north. After announcing the church plant we held an informational meeting for anyone who was interested. The next step was for people to fill out an online interest form. There were about 5 questions aimed at helping us (and them) understand their motives for going. Once we received those, each person/couple/family was interviewed by the church planter or pastors from their sending church. This was a helpful and crucial process for us.

Rather than a 'core team' we called ourselves a 'launch community'. Everyone was a part of this

---

4. Planted from *Covenant Fellowship Church*, Glen Mills, PA.

effort, not just the leadership, and we would need to use all the talents and gifts God had given us to accomplish our goal. That goal was purposefully kept simple: love God, love the world and love each other. This was our hearts' cry and our mission.

The night we passed around ministry team signup sheets I was moved by the response. The front of the room flooded with people, pen in hand, eager to advance the cause of Christ. When the day finally arrived for the group of seventy adults and their families that had committed to leaving the church they had grown to love, I asked them never to call ourselves a 'launch community' again. We weren't a mission team, a core team, or a group of 'insiders' from a different church hoping to make something happen in a new city with new people. We were a fellowship of believers, a local church before we even stepped in the door. Taking our name from a local river, we called ourselves 'Brandywine Grace' from that day forward.

Outreach was central to our mission – and we did a lot of it throughout our first year. But who could have guessed that 3,000 people would show up for our community Easter Egg Hunt? The task of sharing the gospel was ever before us as the greatest story ever told could be heard in all kinds of places – in diners and driveways, in parks and porches, in classrooms and living rooms, on street corners handing out water in the summer heat, in malls wrapping Christmas gifts for busy shoppers, and on sidewalks to strangers searching for hope.

Through events like these and the faithful invitations of our members, we are humbled that the Lord has added 100 people to our fellowship in the first ten months. Looking around on a Sunday morning, it feels more like an established church than a church plant, and we are so grateful for how gracious the Lord has been to Brandywine Grace.

—— Kenny Lynch ——
www.brandywinegrace.org

Grace Church, Birmingham, UK[5]

Grace Church began with thirty-six adults and five kids. We began publicly meeting on an Easter Sunday although we'd had six weeks behind closed doors where we looked at Acts 2 and considered what values and priorities would shape who we were. Before that we had met as home groups under the umbrella of City Church — forming good gospel relationships as we studied, prayed and planned to plant.

There were three of us as elders who led the church. One worked full-time for the church, another part-time and one as a lay elder. As well as these three elders there was an elder from City Church who met with us and prayed, advised and encouraged as well as some very capable deacons whom we consulted.

We began meeting as a '4 o'clock congregation' in a Brethren Gospel Hall. We have a mobile membership who are often away at weekends

5. Planted from *City Church*.

and an afternoon meeting gave folk the chance to come back. It also meant we could do 'Sunday Seminars' in the mornings which involved an opportunity to pray, followed by a choice of six-week tracks looking at various topics.

The ministries that we began near our launch were pretty much decided for us by the community into which God placed us. There were a number of 'lively' youths who had enjoyed terrorizing the Brethren Church who met on Sunday mornings. We started a Monday youth-group for them which is still going strong. This was quickly followed by 'Noah's Ark' (a weekly mums' stay and play) and then Noah's Ark for dads (monthly). These have been great opportunities to build bridges with the local community, as well as to share the gospel.

About nine months into our plant the Brethren Church asked us to take on the running of their family service and so we've been meeting together at 11am. We like to say we began 'courting' and we're probably now 'engaged' and getting closer to 'marriage'! In some senses we're one church but in others we're still two churches with separate but slowly integrating schedules. Culturally we're a little different so, as with any relationship, sensitivity and compromise is necessary but we're thrilled to have the wisdom and experience of senior saints Sunday by Sunday.

----Dan Steel----

www.gracechurchsc.org.uk

Christ Church South Cambs, Sawston, UK[6]

Christ Church South Cambs came into existence after a small Anglican parish church building became too small for its morning congregation. Twelve couples who had mostly been commuting from a nearby village were sent out to plant a new church in that village. It took eighteen months before we moved out of a house into a school and another six months before we were in the school we had been aiming at.

Led by a minister from the parent church, we were mainly young couples with small children and therefore with ample community contacts through neighbours and children. There were initial encouragements from denominational authorities but these dried up when the plant became more than just an idea.

In a village of 7,500 people and with only a tiny percentage involved in either the existing Anglican Church or the Free Church we wanted to be reaching people who didn't normally go to church. We have met at different times of day and settled on Sunday mornings. We have been able to fill a gap in the village by running two successful holiday clubs and have learnt a little of what does and doesn't work in terms of evangelistic events. More food and chatting seem to work, gimmicks and lame excuses for getting in the gospel don't.

We have found it hard staffing children's work on Sundays with tired parents of small children

---

6.   Planted from *All Saints*, Little Shelford.

being our major resource. Being a small and fragile church, what we miss is not having our own building for midweek meetings. What we like is not having our own building to drain us of money in maintenance! If we were to do it again we would pray even harder for a good age range at the start: more older couples and more singles would have given us balance and strength in depth when we needed it.

——Tim Chapman——
www.christchurchsouthcambs.org

Grace Church, Bristol, UK[7]

[Although listed as a mother-daughter plant this could also be seen as a 'start up church' in a new region because the plant was a long way from the mother church.]

Our story begins, not in Bristol, but in South Wales, where the pastors of Christchurch (a large church in the city of Newport, and the first Sovereign Grace church in the UK) had a deep desire to see other gospel-centred churches planted around the country.

After prayerfully searching out a suitable location, Bristol was chosen as somewhere that was near enough to allow Christchurch to offer care and oversight of the new church, and as a city needing more gospel-centred churches.

---

7. Planted from Christchurch, Newport, *Sovereign Grace*.

Having grown up in the church, and sensing a call to pastoral ministry, the pastors of Christchurch evaluated and assessed my call and gift and I was subsequently trained within the Sovereign Grace network before joining the pastoral team at Christchurch with a view to leading this church plant. Over a fifteen month period the vision for the plant was cast and a core group of fifteen adults was gathered from Christchurch. The core group began meeting weekly as a separate small group within the church. We got to know each other, studied together, planned and prayed.

Over a period of time the families and members of this core group all relocated to Bristol. We had already pinpointed an area of the city needy for a gospel-centred church. The new church was advertised locally and then Grace Church opened its doors for Sunday morning services in a school hall. During the first four months a small 'catalyst team' was sent from Christchurch each Sunday morning, to join with the core group, with the purpose of helping with the practicalities of running a Sunday service.

I led the church full-time from the beginning with input from two faithful men, who had both led small groups at the sending church, together with oversight from the sending church pastors. During the first two years major financial support for the church plant came from the Sovereign Grace network.

By God's grace, the church has slowly and steadily grown from those small beginnings to about 110 adults and forty kids. We have experienced the joy of seeing people saved and added to our number, reaching out and serving our wider community, outgrowing our meeting venue and adding a second full-time pastor to our leadership team. And by God's grace, we are still working hard in our mission to build a community of gospel-centred people, who believe, live out and represent the truth of God and His gospel to the world.

—— Nathan Smith——
www.gracechurchbristol.org

3. ON-SITE PLANT
While many churches decide to grow by adding an extra Sunday service (as explained earlier), this model is different in being a new church but on the same premises. This may of course lend itself to a variety of ongoing joint ministry.

Trinity Community Church, Hinckley, UK
We were a middle-sized ordinary Anglican church (about 120 adults and forty kids each Sunday) with a space problem at our morning family service due to growth. We put together a planning group to consider possible ways forward and they arrived at the solution: church planting. This process was well worth the effort, to both own the project and

to know that other options had been discarded with good reason.

The wider church met to consider how this might happen over the course of the next year in large meetings and with much coffee and prayer. After much deliberation we decided to plant a new family-friendly church meeting on the same site in the afternoons. Family, because that's where we were growing. Afternoons, because we wanted to engage with a new group who wouldn't find Sunday morning a great time.

It was a gradual step by step planting. To start with it acted as a separate congregation meeting on-site in the church hall. Over time, as it grew, it established itself as a legal and then financial entity. A core team of just thirteen adults came together to pray. Leadership was from the curate from the original church but two other elders were appointed from within the plant group. We met as a home group for a month and then started Sunday meetings too.

Looking at it so far the trap to avoid was to 'do church' with all the trimmings but with a tenth of the resources. The other constant battle was to work relationally with people rather than fulfil the planned schedule but without falling into disarray. The hardest thing has been for a growing group to grow into a new church culture rather than a convenient pattern.

———Andy Winter———
www.holytrinityhinckley.org.uk

4pm Congregation, Dundonald, Wimbledon, UK
(We earlier drew the distinction between an on-site plant and a second service. This case study falls somewhere between the two, and so provides an interesting example of creating space for growth without creating a fully independent new congregation.)

Dundonald church had a morning and evening congregation but growth in the morning had resulted in growth of a large 'fringe' group, and lack of space for children's ministry. This resulted in discussions about how to create room for further growth.

A traditional 'second service' model was considered. However it was felt it would restrict the relational space available either side of a service and eventually an afternoon congregation was chosen.

Andy Fenton had been leading the evening congregation and he gathered a group of about a dozen people who he knew well who would form the core group of the new congregation. This group began to meet weekly to pray and plan.

It was decided that the new congregation would focus on young families – children's groups would only cater for primary school age and under. A family friendly feel would be cultivated, for example providing a feeding room with video streaming of the service, and the service would be followed by a children's sandwich tea.

The new congregation was announced to the morning and evening congregations and a meeting was held for those who were interested. Meanwhile the core group invited others to consider coming. This resulted in around forty adults who would come at the start. The personnel of this core group was managed by the leadership with several people being asked not to move from other congregations because of greater need there.

After about six months the first Sunday meeting was started and about sixty-five adults came. A year later the congregation is around eighty-five adults with lots of young children.

The relationship with the other Dundonald congregations is 'semi-independent'. Each congregation has its own leadership structure, eldership and small groups. However the senior pastor preaches regularly at each congregation, and the staff team meets together regularly as part of the wider Co-mission network.

—— Andy Fenton ——
www.co-mission.org.uk/ddc

4. HOUSE CHURCH
The first of these is a type of mother-daughter plant; however it was consciously a house church style plant. The second example is that of an established house church planting again.

Urban Life, Derby, UK[8]
The dream that became Urban Life began as my wife Emma and I talked about our future and

---

8.   Planted from *Woodlands Evangelical Church*.

where God might be leading us. I was one of the pastors of a growing church in the affluent suburbs of Derby but two burdens were growing in our minds: the need of our neglected inner cities, and the need to reach the nations of our world – lots of whom live in those inner city areas. Linked to this was a growing conviction that there would be a number of advantages to doing church in a much smaller, simpler, relational way.

It became apparent that a friend was similarly burdened and following some months of thinking and praying we talked with the rest of the church leadership. Together with them we agreed to a plan whereby we would recruit a team from the church who would move into Derby's multicultural inner city. This would be a house church, working as part of the Crowded House network.

We presented our vision to the church members and discussed possible team members with the elders. We approached the people we agreed upon and talked about our vision and values to ensure clarity on the direction of the new church. Over a number of months the team was born. Nine adults and six children were commissioned by Woodlands to form Urban Life.

We had no existing relationships in the area and it took a while for us all to move in; but we asked missionary questions (where do people socialize, what do they do, what are their interests, what are their needs, how can we serve them?) and soon friendships began to build.

One year on we are involved with community life in a variety of ways: chatting in the pub, watching football in a local Kurdish café, meeting up in local parks, hosting lunches for Pakistani women, volunteering in a council day centre, helping an alcoholic find rehab, teaching English language classes, starting an 'English Corner' conversation club, and reading the bible with interested friends. In all these things we aim to work with the grain of a local culture where people are highly unlikely to come to us – so we are going to them.

———Anthony Adams———
www.thecrowdedhouse.org

The Crowded House 'Abbey' Congregation, Sheffield, UK

The Crowded House (TCH) is a network of missional churches. TCH Sharrow was one of these churches and it was time for it to multiply: we'd grown to over thirty and were running out of space. Not just physical space, as we squeezed into a home for our meetings, but relational space. We have a strong commitment to mission through community and we were finding it hard to share our lives with everyone in the group plus their unbelieving contacts.

Dividing up a close group is painful. There have been some tears every time we've done it. But 'growing by planting' is written into our vision and people are up for it. Indeed this time round I had to put the brakes on because two of the new leaders had just got married and we wanted to give them a year before they took on new responsibilities. When we multiplied, I led one group with a new, young leader to give him the space to grow into leadership. We also talked about both groups planting: we were creating two new congregations rather than sending out a new congregation from an old one.

As best we could, we tried to create two new groups with a mix of personalities and shared ministry interests. You can't do everything when you're a small church so both groups had a clear focus for their mission. There are three strands to our approach to evangelism: building relationships, sharing the gospel and introducing people to the Christian community. So both groups began by talking about who they wanted to reach, how they could build relationships, how they could contextualize the gospel and what communal activities they could invite people to. We want people to see the love of Christ in our life together (John 13:34-5). It's real life, warts-and-all exposure, but that's okay because we're witnesses to grace, not good works.

—Tim Chester—
www.thecrowdedhouse.org

5. MULTI-SITE CHURCH

Multi-site churches are relatively rare in the UK but here is one example.

St Ebbe's, in Headington, Oxford, UK

St Ebbe's is an evangelical Anglican church in the centre of Oxford. The evening service had reached capacity in terms of numbers: there was no room for growth, and therefore a real risk of 'plateauing out'. The best solution to this was not to address the size or layout of the building, but to look outward and off-site.

The reasons for planting began to gather:

* A good number of those at the evening service lived in the east of the city;

* Those suburbs have thousands of residents, but only a small number of Bible-teaching churches;

* We wanted to see the gospel advance at Brookes University with 18,000 students living across East Oxford.

Discussions followed with the Bishop of Oxford and others; and within St Ebbe's too. We began meeting in a school in Headington taking sixty or so volunteers out of the 6.30pm congregation, under the leadership of a full-time staff member, with two apprentices.

Subsequent changes:

- After three years we added a morning congregation.

- After five years, in a remarkable answer to prayer, we bought a building.

- After eight years we added on an afternoon congregation.

These congregations are described as part of St Ebbe's Church: for example for a long time there was joint finance and the leadership at central St Ebbe's has retained a degree of oversight over the plant. It also has clearly had the St Ebbe's 'badge'. However as time has gone on the plant has started to function more independently and further steps may be taken in that direction.

—Al Horn—
www.stebbes.org.uk

6. NETWORK COLLABORATION

Networks operate in different ways. Here we have two examples of a 'local' network, and then several examples of a 'national' network.

Christ Church, Balham, London, UK[9]

Balham is an inner city suburb; a strange hybrid of inner city and suburbia. The majority of people

---

9. *Co-Mission network*

are in their 20s and educated to degree level. The place is full of bars and restaurants. Some families stay for a while but 'middle class white flight' takes over in the early primary school years.

A group of approximately twenty-five people launched Christ Church Balham as an evening congregation in a school hall. We were sent by Dundonald Church, Wimbledon part of the Co-Mission network of churches. We recognized that we were young (most in our 20s), I was inexperienced having come straight from theological college, and we were few in number. There were many things that we could not do on our own. We felt vulnerable but the support we received from Co-Mission was invaluable in helping us to grow. Co-Mission helped with training our small group leaders, experienced ministers were available for encouragement and we would periodically gather together for courses or larger events.

Principally we were a 'network' church plant. Though a handful of the initial crowd lived in Balham, many did not. We were an eclectic group who were connected not so much by geography but by friendship networks. Balham enjoys good transport links and so we hoped to grow by accessing our friends through those networks in a place that was easily accessible to them.

We weren't especially well thought through. We've learnt as we've gone along. We simply knew that we had a small crowd, a place to meet, some musicians, a Bible and a great God. And so we were prepared to give it a go. In His kindness,

God has given us modest growth, some of it through conversion but not nearly enough!

——Richard Perkins——
www.christchurchbalham.org.uk

St John's Chelsea, London, UK[10]

St John's, Chelsea started as a mission initiative based in an empty Anglican church building on the World's End Estate in central London. The World's End is an area of about 5,000 people, with three main estates and comprising a huge range of ethnic/national diversity. St John's Church is located on the estate but had had no sustained local congregation for over twenty years.

The project started as a co-operation between a sister church and the Co-mission initiative (which has provided funding and oversight). I was called to initiate/pastor the work and so set about recruiting a team of volunteers to get involved and meet to pray. One of the big challenges we faced in terms of recruitment was that our support base was mainly Christian young professionals in Co-mission congregations. This was a completely different demographic to the one we were trying to reach, so there was a great danger that any initial congregation would implicitly 'exclude' the very people we were trying to reach. Further, none of them lived locally – something which we believed was essential to having any integrity in doing outreach.

---

10. *Co-Mission network*

Therefore, we kept the group deliberately small (fifteen to twenty people) and sought to work towards a long term goal of getting some people to move locally. We met to pray and discuss our vision in the months before we tried to launch any services and I spent time getting to know the area and local individuals. Thankfully, over time we have been able to become a socially diverse congregation and a number of people have moved into the local area.

The vision for our ministry has been to be a 'church for people who don't go to church'. So, we have deliberately shaped what we do to make things relevant and understandable for the outsider as we have wanted to grow through conversions and not by recruiting people from other churches.

——Andy Mason——
www.stjohnschelsea.wordpress.com

Gateway Church, Wrexham, UK[11]

Gateway Church started with the Newfrontiers team in the West Midlands feeling the need of the church in Wales and pinpointing Wrexham as a strategic place to plant a church. They approached Nigel and Cally Lloyd who were leaving Rugeley Community Church to go to Wrexham.

Nigel and Cally visited Wrexham, met with church leaders there and discussed the proposed

---

11. *Newfrontiers*

plant with Newfrontiers. They decided to make the move – with the personal cost of a daughter staying behind to finish A levels, an unknown future and no financial support.

Once in Wrexham Nigel and Cally began by praying together as a family – specifically that God would bring people to build the church. A small group began to form. Some were local people who had heard of the proposed plant; some people from within the Newfontiers network who gradually moved from elsewhere in the country.

At these meetings the vision and values for the plant church were presented as well as ongoing prayer. This group became too large for a house and began to meet in a hired hall on Tuesday evenings. This meeting was advertised around Wrexham resulting in more interest being shown.

Starting from scratch in this way meant that these meetings were presenting people with a vision of what might be, rather than inviting them to join something currently in existence. Some who showed initial interest during this time ended up not being part of the plant.

By the end of the first year there were about twenty-five people who were committed to the new church and so a new structure was launched: Sunday morning meetings were started, and the mid-week meeting became two small groups. There was also a Sunday evening prayer meeting.

Three and half years later the congregation is around sixty adults plus children. A core leadership of three has been formed, along with a wider leadership team. And now a daughter church is being planned.

—Nigel Lloyd—
www.gatewaychurchwrexham.org.uk

Emmanuel Church, Oxford, UK[12]

Emmanuel Church, Oxford began by way of a conversation about raising up young men and women in University cities who could influence our nation in a godly way through their likely future careers. It was noted that there was no Newfrontiers church in Oxford and it was suggested to David and Margaret Coak that they move to Oxford to pioneer a new work.

Information about the proposed plant was circulated within the Newfrontiers network of churches. This resulted in about half a dozen people from around the country expressing their desire to be involved in the new work. It was also shared at David and Margaret's home church in Cambridge with the result that about nine people decided to join the core group. One person was also specifically asked from a church in Norwich to join the plant to be part of the leadership team.

A meeting was organized in Oxford to advertise and discuss the proposed plant. This resulted in a number of people already in the city, and from elsewhere, hearing of the plans and expressing

12. *Newfrontiers*

interest in joining. Meetings also took place with other church leaders in the city.

The core group then began to meet together in Oxford about once a month to pray together and to develop their vision for the plant. The focus of the vision was to be a loving community, to keep the Word of God central, to see the Spirit at work, to be committed to training, and to keep prayer at the heart of their life together. We wanted to serve the city of Oxford, see people coming to know Christ, and also contribute to the worldwide spread of the gospel in word and deed

These meetings went on for about a year and then Sunday morning meetings were started. Most of the core group had arrived by this point but some continued to join over the following months resulting in a total of about twenty-five adults.

For the first year or so the meetings of the church involved this Sunday morning meeting plus prayer meetings; after that a small group structure was also formed. Four years later the church has about 140 adults and three full time staff.

——David Coak——
www.emmanueloxford.org

Jubilee Church, Hull, UK[13]

Steve Whittington was a pastor of a Newfrontiers church in Teesside. He and his wife felt a call to church planting but weren't sure where that

---

13. *Newfrontiers*

should be. He knew that a Newfrontiers church in York were praying for the city of Hull and went to their prayer meetings. Eventually they felt God tell them they should look to plant in Hull.

They began to recruit a core team. Some came from their home church in Teesside; they also asked contacts from elsewhere to come to serve in specific ways, e.g. a worship leader from Brighton. The proposed plant was also advertised within Newfrontiers circles. All of this resulted in a core team of thirteen adults.

Funding was available from Newfrontiers for a full-time pastor's salary for the first eighteen months. In addition churches in the region and the home church in Teesside gave financial support – particularly for a variety of set up costs.

Steve and his family moved to Hull and started making a variety of contacts through work situations, street evangelism, and advertising in the local Christian bookshop. The result was a core group of about thirty people. Over a couple of months they met together to get to know each other and to pray for the city. Then they started meeting together on a Sunday morning using a hired church hall. At first these meetings focused on setting out the vision and values of the church.

They also started mid-week meetings which were aimed at prayer and training in evangelism. This mid-week meeting then became an Alpha course for the whole church and any contacts they had. In God's goodness they saw people come to faith very early in their life together. After three months they needed to move to a larger venue.

They also began doing practical work on the estate they were based on, such as public clear ups. The church has been very ethnically mixed (about forty per cent non-white British). This has been recognized and encouraged in practical ways such as singing in a variety of languages. Three and half years later they are a congregation of 110 adults and about forty kids.

——Steve Whittington——
www.notdull.org

City Church, Dundee, UK

Prophetic birth
In February 2005 about fifteen folks from Dundee attended a 'Scotland Day' hosted by New-frontiers in Edinburgh. The day was focused on praying for great churches to be established in Scotland, and this included a time of prayer for Dundee. As we prayed, David Holden prophesied, "that God would establish a church founded on grace in a city built on the law". Not many people knew that Dundee is built on an extinct volcano called 'The Law', or that we had been battling with a legalistic church outlook!

Good Foundations

We started to travel through to a Newfrontiers church in neighbouring Perth to learn and understand the values of good church. Leaders from other Newfrontiers churches in Scotland helped with teaching on vital areas. We then launched in January 2006 with a congregation of about forty people. We have striven to be a 'Biblical Church' making it very clear that scripture has final authority in all we do.

A Sovereign Father

Although we have worked hard, the story of City Church has been one of God's sovereignty. We were not "ambitious", we simply wanted to serve God and have a church in Dundee that would honour His Word and seek the presence of God by His Spirit. The list of things we didn't have was certainly bigger than the list of talents! In fact we even started without a clearly identified leader, that coming some eight months into the plant, in some ways this was the 'wrong way round' but it meant we were built around values, not personality.

A Loving, Hospitable Community

We are reformed in doctrine and charismatic in practice, but one of our highest values has always been to be a loving community — it is what has held us together through the first years. We practiced (and practiced!) hospitality, eating together as often as possible. The glue of love in the community has taken us through four years of steady, if not dramatic, growth. If there is one thing that I could advise church planters from our experience it would be to 'love one another'.

If God has told you to church plant, do it with all your heart, it is difficult but glorious!

——Craig Stocks——
www.citychurchdundee.org

7. RE-START CHURCH
These are all situations where an existing church was revitalized or 're-planted' in some way. But they vary greatly in how much that changed the original church (in one case it was closed down for a while) where the plant group came from, and what the resulting church looked like.

Guilford Baptist Church, Sterling, VA, USA
I was on staff as a church planter at Capitol Hill Baptist Church in Washington, DC. The elders at CHBC had decided to begin planting churches to help alleviate the over-crowding there and establish healthy congregations in the fast-growing suburbs. We decided to plant in Sterling, a Virginia suburb about 45 minutes outside of the city. Sterling is located in what was the fastest growing and wealthiest county in America. The area had transformed in the previous decade from a rural community to a busy suburb.

In getting to know the churches in the area, we came across Guilford Baptist Church. GBC never adjusted to the changes in the community around it and was essentially dead. There had been no pastor for over a year, attendance was around ten people most Sundays, and the facilities were in shambles. So, instead of beginning a new work in the backyard of a dying church, we decided to bring our church planting team out to join with the people at Guilford. The team consisted of eight people and myself, all members of Capitol Hill Baptist who lived in the Sterling area or who were willing to move. They were all self-selected; we just asked who wanted to come, and these eight people did. In retrospect, some were more suited for church planting than others. I think I should have been more proactive in recruiting gifted people and urging them to invest themselves in the church plant.

It was rocky at first (half of the 'old' Guilford members left within the first few months), but over time people began to love each other and grasp a passion for seeing the gospel spread. The sending church had committed to providing financial support for three years (100 per cent the first year, 50 per cent the second year, 25 per cent the third year), but Guilford grew steadily and was able to sustain itself after just a year or so. We were able to appoint elders and deacons after about eighteen months.

We haven't implemented many programs, but rather we focus our congregational life around the systematic preaching of God's word and genuine community. We've seen lives transformed and a 'real' church take shape over the past five years. We now meet in a school (having outgrown the church's little chapel) and have planted two churches for Spanish speakers in the area.

———Mike McKinley———
www.guilfordbc.org

Speke Baptist Church, Liverpool, UK[14]

Speke is amongst the most severely deprived housing estates in the country, with escalating drug-related violent crime and arson. There is a strong sense of community identity and genuine warmth. Following an initiative to bus kids living in Speke four miles to a kids' club at a large independent evangelical church (Bridge Chapel), a small but passionate team started looking for a place within Speke to run a Gospel-centred kids' and families' outreach.

Unknown to them Speke Baptist church, made up of a dwindling number of senior praying saints who mainly lived outside the area, had been praying for a new generation to come to the church to rejuvenate the Gospel work. As a result for a couple of years a new kids' club was started in their property. This eventually gave way to a team being formally sent to form a new Sunday morning congregation made up of approximately fifteen from both the existing congregation and sending church.

---

14. planted into from *Bridge Chapel*

Effectively we had a new church in an existing building. Over the next year members of the team from Bridge Chapel both moved into the area and took over leadership responsibilities within the church. A pastor was appointed from within, along with a community outreach worker, to support the strategy of trying to visit families, teens, schools, and seniors' homes in order to build relationships of trust.

The progress was frustratingly slow and growth has been hard fought, however, something of a breakthrough in interest and acceptance was experienced when some of the church members' own children started attending local schools. Conversions have come, by God's grace, through the parent ministry attached to the kids' club, the football team, seniors' Christianity Explored and teens' outreach. In addition, the Lord has drawn many backslidden and hurting believers in Speke to the church family to be equipped and discipled. The resultant growth has brought us to the point where we have recently purchased the local pub to convert into a church building and centre for community outreach.

— Steve Casey—
www.spekebaptistchurch.org.uk

Holywood Baptist Church, Holywood, Northern Ireland, UK[15]

Holywood is a town of around 12,000 five miles east of Belfast. The church there dwindled to the

---

15. planted into from *Strandtown Baptist Church*

point where it was difficult to sustain an effective ministry. So on the retirement of their part time pastor, the leaders approached Strandtown Baptist Church in Belfast to ask for help. Several meetings took place between the leaders of the two churches and it was eventually proposed that they would merge with the view to re-establishing the Holywood church at some time in the future.

The stated vision was 'To see Holywood Baptist Church re-established as a vibrant and independent worshipping and witnessing community, serving the people of the town'. This merger was approved by the members of both congregations.

The leaders from Holywood joined with those from Strandtown, the finances were pooled and the combined church was imaginatively named Holywood/Strandtown Baptist Church! This combined church then met at Strandtown; no services were held in the Holywood building although some youth work was still located there. During the following months the congregation prayerfully considered the way forward.

Just over a year later a morning service recommenced in Holywood with about fifty people from the combined church, including two of the elders. The two pastors at Strandtown preached at both churches. The Holywood church gradually began to grow until, another year on about 120 people were meeting and they relocated to a Leisure Centre. One of the elders who had moved with the group to Holywood became the full time pastor. A combined service still took place in the evening at Strandtown and one leadership team still oversaw the work of both churches.

The Holywood church gradually began to function more independently of Strandtown and five years after the merger Holywood Baptist Church was formally reconstituted as an independent church. The church now has its own leaders and pastor and is financially independent.

——Alistair McNeice——
www.holywoodbaptist.org.uk

Moorlands Evangelical Church, Lancaster, UK

While investigating the possibility of church planting in Lancaster we discovered a small Brethren assembly that was closing due to dwindling numbers. After sharing our vision with them and considering various options we agreed that I should be appointed as the pastor of the tiny church as a means to establishing the new work. We had recruited a core team to join with us – these were people we knew who we asked to consider moving to Lancaster to help, or people we were put in contact with through publicizing the venture.

The original church family consisted of a dozen, mainly elderly, people, and with my family and core team we'd formed we had a congregation of around twenty from the beginning and a small building in which to meet. This felt immediately like a viable church which made it easier for people to join. Furthermore we hoped that the church's seventy-five year 'heritage' and reputation in the city would help us avoid controversy and hostility among other churches, and suspicion among the people we were hoping to reach.

The original members of the Brethren assembly understood that change would have to be dramatic: it needed a complete new start or face a slow death. However the loss of comfort and control for some of the original members was too much and half of them left within the first year. This was very traumatic for everyone and in that first year the alternative option of starting from scratch seemed much more attractive! Meanwhile the hostility and suspicion from other local churches that we hoped to minimize by keeping the name of Moorlands was in fact apparent from the start and has grown as we have grown.

However, with hindsight, I think three advantages outweigh these costs. Firstly the benefits of inheriting a building and small congregation are probably short term, but can provide a very practical head start in a virgin territory church plant. Secondly being rooted in the history of a place is worth more, evangelistically, than we expected. Finally one of the greatest joys for us has been seeing those few folk from the original church who stayed on become spiritually renewed as they have prayed, served and rejoiced with us at the growth God has graciously given.

——Danny Rurlander——
www.moorlands.org.uk

The Crowded House, Sharrowvale, Sheffield, UK

Existing churches and the buildings they meet in have the potential to offer a great opportunity for church planting. They already have a 'place' in the local area and have resources that can be put to good gospel use. It was recognition of this potential that led a household congregation that was part of The Crowded House in Sheffield to close down and move into an established but rapidly declining church.

This was a good example of 'out of the box' thinking. Being a household church of twenty mainly young adults gave almost limitless freedom and flexibility. Getting involved with an established, but declining church, with an average age of 65+ and all the attendant cherished practices and traditions, didn't seem the most rational decision! But it has proved to be a wise, gospel strategy resulting in the planting of a number of churches.

There were three key attitudes in place that meant the decision was not so foolhardy after all.

(1) Stark realism

The folk in the established church knew that they had five years at the most. Their situation was terminal. It was major, invasive surgery that was needed rather than a sticking plaster. This has meant that radical changes were not only necessary but also accepted.

(2) Gospel conviction

The people in the established church did not want to close the doors for the last time because they did not want the area to lose the gospel witness. Those in the household church recognized the gospel opportunity the re-plant offered.

(3) Steady determination

Even with everything in place, the transition has been far from painless. But a task was undertaken and by grace a genuine transformation has taken place. Leadership is a case in point. It was a carefully managed transition involving three deliberate steps:

1. I worked with the existing leadership from the established church.

2. That leadership team was slimmed down over a 12 month period.

3. A formal eldership was recognized which did not involve any of the previous leaders.

Significantly, no one left as a result of the thorough-going leadership changes. Now, the building is full each week; active gospel communities are operating around the city; people have become Christians; the local area is being served with, for example, music cafés for local musicians, exhibitions for local artists, parent and toddler groups, luncheon clubs for the elderly and language classes for asylum seekers and refugees.

— Steve Timmis —
www.thecrowdedhouse.org

Resources and Further Reading

BOOKS ON CHURCH AND CHURCH PLANTING

- *Church Planter Manual*. Timothy J Keller & J Allen Thompson. Available from Redeemer Church Planting Center.

- *Total Church: a radical re-shaping around gospel and community*. Tim Chester & Steve Timmis (IVP, 2007).

- *Planting Churches – Changing Communities: A hands-on guide to successful church planting*. David Stroud (Authentic, 2009).

- *Multiplying Churches: reaching today's communities through church planting*. Edited by Steve Timmis (Christian Focus, 2000).

- *Church Planting is for Wimps: How God Uses Messed-Up People to Plant Ordinary Churches*

That Do Extraordinary Things. Mike McKinley (Crossway, 2010).

- *God's New Community: New Testament patterns for today's church*. Graham Beynon (IVP, 2005).

LEGAL AND FINANCIAL ADVICE

- Stewardship (www.stewardship.org.uk)
- Fellowship of Evangelical Churches (www.fiec.org.uk)

SOME CHURCH PLANTING GROUPS AND NETWORKS

- www.co-mission.org.uk
- www.acts29network.org
- www.redeemercitytocity.com
- www.ukchurchplanting.org
- www.thecrowdedhouse.org

A NOTE ON THE ACTS 29 NETWORK:

The Acts 29 Network exists to start churches that plant churches. The network originates in the USA with the vision being to band together Christian, Evangelical, Missional and Reformed churches, who, for the sake of Jesus and the gospel, plant churches across the United States and the world.

In May 2009 Steve Timmis was appointed to the role of Director of Acts 29 Western Europe, signifying the formal launch of Acts 29 in that area of the world. The remit for Acts 29 Western Europe is simple: it exists to help people and churches plant churches that plant churches. That help involves:

1. An excellent assessment process that helps people or churches make wise decisions about planting.

2. A good coaching structure providing support from those more experienced in planting churches.

3. Access to a helpful training programme delivered through The Porterbrook Network, which is biblical and missional.

4. A well-established peer-to-peer support network.

Acts 29 does not seek to own church plants or even support only one model of church planting. It aims to 'merely' facilitate the planting of gospel centred churches and provide on-going support for a person or church's vision.

Why Join a small Church? →
John Benton

Why Join a Small Church

JOHN BENTON

To join a big and thriving church is not always wrong, but it is frequently the easy option. To join a little, needy congregation is not a decision to be taken lightly. It will probably require far more guts, love, resilience and spiritual exertion. But how the devil would love to herd Christians into a few big city centre churches, getting them to travel miles from their communities, and leaving vast tracts of our country with no viable witness for the gospel.

This book is written as a plea for Christians to think again about getting involved with a small church. Ask yourself the question, 'How can we drive past one church to go to another?'

John Benton is pastor of Chertsey Street Baptist Church, Guildford, England and Managing Editor of the monthly newspaper, Evangelicals Now. John & his wife Ann have written many books; some as a joint venture. They are in demand as conference speakers.

ISBN 978-1-84550-407-6

ORLANDO SAER

IRON
SHARPENS
IRON

Leading Bible-Oriented Small Groups that Thrive

"It is terrific, truly the best book of its kind I have ever read."
R. Kent Hughes, Senior Pastor Emeritus, College Church, Wheaton, Illinois

Iron Sharpens Iron
Leading Bible-Oriented Small Groups that Thrive

ORLANDO SAER

It's the best material I've read on small group bible study leading and would be useful both for someone leading their first bible study and for someone who's been leading bible studies for decades.

9 Marks Blog

Iron Sharpens Iron! Small Bible-study groups are great places for Christians both to interact with God's Word and to share their lives with others. They provide relaxed and informal settings which facilitate growth in grace and understanding. Orlando Saer provides a realistic and practical guide for anyone leading or wanting to lead such a group. This book will give you the tools you need as a leader to see your group thrive.

Orlando Saer is Senior Minister of Cranleigh Baptist Church in Surrey. He has been involved in leading small groups and training other leaders for almost twenty years. Formerly a teacher, he is married to Libby and they have four children.

ISBN 978-1-84550-575-2

The reality of

encountering Jesus

Rich
The Reality of Encountering Jesus

PETER DICKSON AND DAVID GIBSON

Not a safe book. Peter Dickson is a bit sneaky (the book is so engagingly written) and yet terribly stubborn (he refuses to offer you a bland, smooth, mass-market, shrink-wrapped Jesus). So reading it may make you savingly angry or fearfully grateful–either of which will be okay. I find so refreshing this combination of contemporary clarity and old, rugged gospel.

Dale Ralph Davis
Well-respected author and Bible expositor

What does it mean to belong to God's family? Consider the gospel of Luke which introduces us to Jesus the most important man who ever lived. This book demonstrates that encountering Jesus is a matter of urgency for all people everywhere. The Gospel of Luke is applied to a 21st century audience using contemporary illustrations including the recent financial crisis.

Peter Dickson has been minister at High Church, Hilton in Aberdeen since 1996. He grew up in Edinburgh and St. Andrews and became a Christian through the witness of Scripture Union camps. He is married to Eleanor, who comes from Inverness, and they have two children, Esther and Jamie.

David Gibson was born in America and grew up in East Africa and Northern Ireland. He has a Ph.D in Theology from the University of Aberdeen and is currently the Assistant Minister at High Church, Hilton. Married to Angela, his interests include writing, playing football, watching rugby, entertaining and being entertained by his children, Archie, Ella and Samuel.

ISBN 978-1-84550-607-0

Christian Focus Publications
publishes books for all ages

Our mission statement –

STAYING FAITHFUL
In dependence upon God we seek to impact the world through literature faithful to His infallible Word, the Bible. Our aim is to ensure that the Lord Jesus Christ is presented as the only hope to obtain forgiveness of sin, live a useful life and look forward to heaven with Him.

REACHING OUT
Christ's last command requires us to reach out to our world with His gospel. We seek to help fulfill that by publishing books that point people towards Jesus and help them develop a Christ-like maturity. We aim to equip all levels of readers for life, work, ministry and mission.

Books in our adult range are published in three imprints:

Christian Focus contains popular works including bio-graphies, commentaries, basic doctrine and Christian living. Our children's books are also published in this imprint.

Mentor focuses on books written at a level suitable for Bible College and seminary students, pastors, and other serious readers. The imprint includes commentaries, doctrinal studies, examination of current issues and church history.

Christian Heritage contains classic writings from the past.

Christian Focus Publications, Ltd
Geanies House, Fearn, Ross-shire,
IV20 1TW, Scotland, United Kingdom
www.christianfocus.com